CHRISTIAN HITS for TEENS

8 GRADED SELECTIONS
FOR INTERMEDIATE TO LATE INTERMEDIATE PIANISTS
ARRANGED BY MELODY BOBER

Each generation has its unique style of musical worship to immerse individuals in praise and thanksgiving. Such music helps increase faith and leads toward a closer walk with God. Soulful melodies can extol God's love, provision, and comfort, and lyrics can touch hearts.

Christian Hits for Teens contains solo piano arrangements that students from this generation will recognize and enjoy learning. These familiar praise and worship songs, with their rhythmic vitality and rich harmonies, will especially appeal to teens. Students will enjoy performing these pieces at youth groups, camps, and in other church settings.

CONTENTS

Produced by
Alfred Music
P.O. Box 10003
Van Nuys, CA 91410-0003
alfred.com

ISBN-10: 1-4706-1120-1
ISBN-13: 978-1-4706-1120-0

Blue polygonal pattern: © Shutterstock.com / ilyianne • Headphones: © Shutterstock.com / Alexander Demyanenko

COURAGEOUS

Words and Music by
Matthew West and Mark Hall
Arr. Melody Bober

With confidence ($\bullet$ = 80)

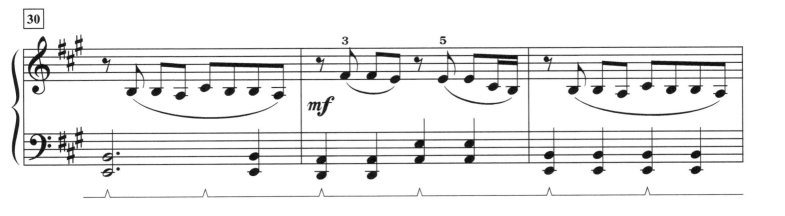

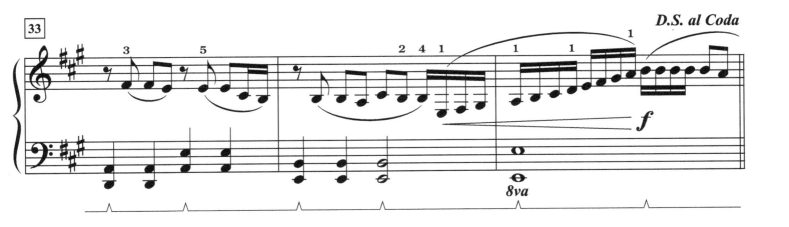

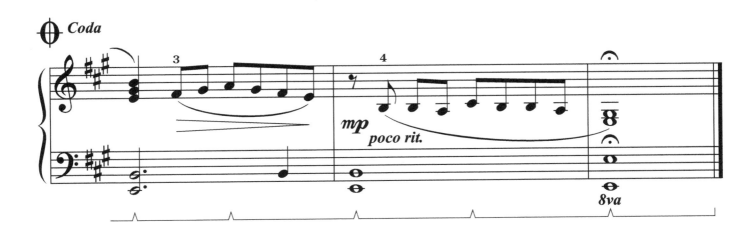

HOW BEAUTIFUL

Words and Music by Twila Paris
Arr. Melody Bober

OCEANS (WHERE FEET MAY FAIL)

Words and Music by Joel Houston,
Matt Crocker, and Salomon Lighthelm
Arr. Melody Bober

I CAN ONLY IMAGINE

Words and Music by Bart Millard
Arr. Melody Bober

REDEEMED

Words and Music by
Benji Cowart and Michael Weaver
Arr. Melody Bober

REVELATION SONG

By Jennie Lee Riddle
Arr. Melody Bober

WHAT A SAVIOR

Words and Music by Jeremiah Jones
Arr. Melody Bober

YOU RAISE ME UP

Words and Music by
Rolf Lovland and Brendan Graham
Arr. Melody Bober